AnimalWays

Ants

AnimalWays

Ants

PAUL FLEISHER

BENCHMARK BOOKS

MARSHALL CAVENDISH
NEW YORK

With thanks to Paul Zabarauskas,
Department of Entomology, Wildlife Conservation Society, New York,
for his expert reading of this manuscript.

Benchmark Books
Marshall Cavendish Corporation
99 White Plains Road
Tarrytown, NY 10591-9001
Website: www.marshallcavendish.com

Library of Congress Cataloging-in-Publication Data
Fleisher, Paul.
Ants / by Paul Fleisher.
p. cm.—(Animalways)
Includes bibliographical references and an index (p. 101).
ISBN 0-7614-1269-7
1. Ants—Juvenile literature. p[1. Ants.] I. Title. II. Series
QL568.F7 F53   2001   595.79'6—dc21   00-065140

Photo Research by Candlepants, Inc.

Cover Photo: *Photo Researchers* / J. H. Robinson

The photographs in this book are used by permission and through the courtesy of *Peter
Arnold*: Allan Morgan, 15 (top); Hans Pfletschinger, 16, 28 (bottom), 62, 63, 68; Darlyne A.
Murawski, 38; David Scharf, 41; Kevin Schafer, 75; M. & C. Photography, 79; *Art Resource*:
Giraudon, 17; *Animals Animals/Earth Scenes*: E. H. Degginger, 21; R. F. Head, 24 (right);
Cooke, J. A. L. OSF, 35; Donald Specker, 47; Raymond A. Mendez, 50, 60, 64, 71; K. G.
Preston-Mafham, 69; Alan G. Nelson, 72; Clyne, D. OSF, 90; Juan Manuel Renjifo, 98;
Brown, J. OSF, back cover; *Photo Researchers*: Gregory G. Dimijian, title page, 24 (left), 29,
66, 76, 81, 87, 88, 93; J. H. Robinson, 9; Nigel J. Dennis, 11; Kenneth H. Thomas, 12, 49;
James H. Robinson, 14 (top), 54 (top), 59; R. J. Erwin, 14 (middle); David T. Roberts
Nature's Images, Inc., 14 (bottom), 51, 78 (bottom); Scott Camazine, 15 (bottom), 45, 67,
83; Dr. Frieder Sauer / Okapia, 18; Biophoto Associates, 26; A. H. Rider, 28 (top); Gary
Retherford, 33, 78 (top), 85; Dr. Paul A. Zahl, 36; Varin/Jacana, 42, 91; Harry Rogers, 46; N.
H. (Dan) Cheatham, 55; S. J. Krasemann, 56; Jacques Jangoux, 58; Grace Thompson, 95;
John Dommers, 100; Peter G. Aitken, 102; *Corbis*: Wolfgang Kaehler, 54 (bottom).

Printed in Italy
1 3 5 6 4 2

Contents

HERE ARE SOME OF THE MAIN PHYLA, CLASSES, AND ORDERS, WITH PHOTOGRAPHS OF A TYPICAL ANIMAL FROM EACH GROUP.

Animal Kingdom

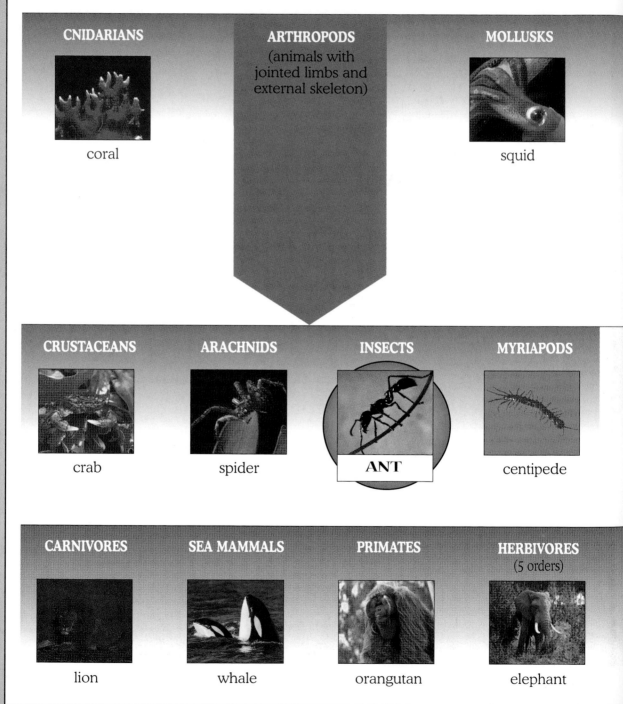

CNIDARIANS

coral

ARTHROPODS
(animals with jointed limbs and external skeleton)

MOLLUSKS

squid

CRUSTACEANS

crab

ARACHNIDS

spider

INSECTS

ANT

MYRIAPODS

centipede

CARNIVORES

lion

SEA MAMMALS

whale

PRIMATES

orangutan

HERBIVORES
(5 orders)

elephant

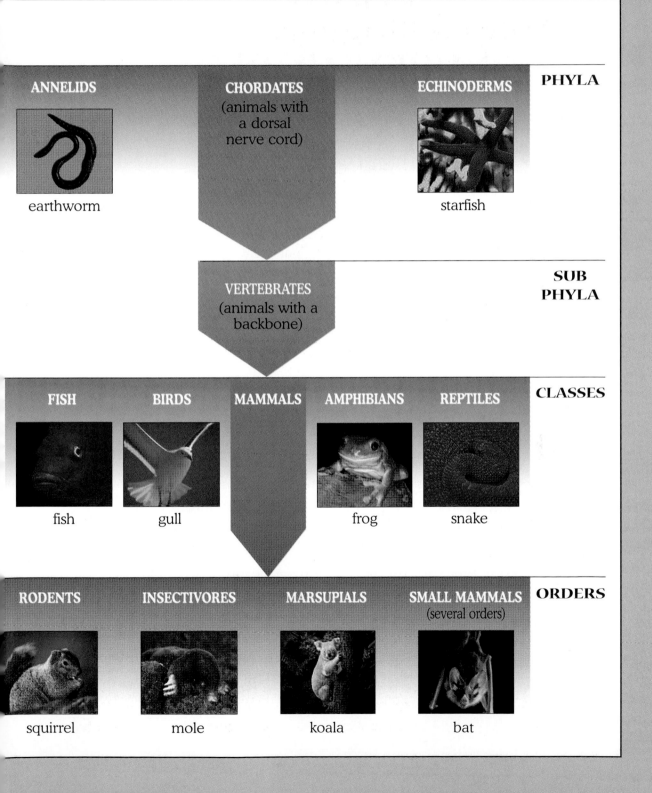

PHYLA

ANNELIDS

earthworm

CHORDATES
(animals with
a dorsal
nerve cord)

ECHINODERMS

starfish

**SUB
PHYLA**

VERTEBRATES
(animals with a
backbone)

CLASSES

FISH

fish

BIRDS

gull

MAMMALS

AMPHIBIANS

frog

REPTILES

snake

ORDERS

RODENTS

squirrel

INSECTIVORES

mole

MARSUPIALS

koala

SMALL MAMMALS
(several orders)

bat

1 They're Everywhere!

A column of large black ants races past the tufts of dry grass on the African plains. They are following a scent trail laid down by a scout ant just minutes earlier. The trail leads to a small hole in a towering earthen mound—home to a huge colony of termites. The ants begin an organized attack. Some of them battle with termite soldiers guarding the opening. Meanwhile, others dart into the termites' nest. Soon they reappear, their jaws full of captured white termite workers.

The ants, which are all females, enter the nest repeatedly. Some carry out termite after termite, while others fight the termite soldiers to the death. Then, as quickly as it started, the raid is over. Each ant gathers up as many termites as she can. The raiding ants rush back to their own colony with their prey, leaving half a dozen dead nestmates behind.

The brain of an ant is microscopic in size. No individual ant leads the colony and makes decisions about how it should be

LOOK CLOSELY AND YOU'LL FIND ANTS LIVING ALMOST EVERYWHERE ON EARTH.

run. Nevertheless, ant colonies are organized and efficient. Whatever needs to be done gets done. The colony grows, feeds itself, raises its young, and reproduces to establish new colonies. In this book you'll find out how these amazing creatures have managed to become one of the most successful groups of living creatures on Earth.

Ant Numbers

There are very few places on Earth where you cannot find ants. They are one of the most widespread of all living creatures. Ants are found on every continent except Antarctica. They live in rain forests and in the driest deserts. They burrow deep underground and build nests high in the treetops. They live in huge numbers in hot tropical regions, but they also live above the Arctic Circle and in cold mountain environments. They live far from human habitation and in the middle of our biggest cities.

Ants are small and quiet. They usually live hidden from sight. So it's not surprising that most people don't realize how important they are in the web of life. Yet ants are among the most dominant animals on Earth. This is not an exaggeration. Imagine you could weigh all the animals in an acre of Amazon rain forest. Almost one-third of the entire weight would be ants! An insect census would find as many ants as all other insects combined. Each acre of rain forest is home to more than three million ants—about seventy-five ants per square foot. A study of ants in Africa's Ivory Coast estimated an even larger population—more than eight million ants per acre.

Along with the other social insects—bees, wasps, and termites—ants dominate the insect world. Dr. Edward O. Wilson, the world's leading authority on ants, estimates there are about ten quadrillion ants (10,000,000,000,000,000) living on our planet

ANTS HAVE BUILT THESE MOUNDS IN THE KALAHARI DESERT OF SOUTHERN AFRICA.

at any one time. That's about 1.5 million ants for each man, woman, and child.

If you were able to weigh all the ants in the world, you'd find they make up about ten percent of all animal life by weight. If you could put all the world's people on one side of a scale, and all the ants on the other, the two sides of the scale would be about balanced.

Several species, or kinds, of ants are so adaptable they have spread around the globe, living almost everywhere on Earth that humans do. In cold climates, ants hibernate deep in their nests through the winter. Desert-dwelling ants forage at night or

Ants are small, but their numbers are great.

when the sun is low, and seek shelter during the hottest part of the day. In times of drought, they dig deep underground to find moisture or avoid heat. Ants can survive huge doses of radiation that would kill most other animals. They have been on Earth 100 million years longer than humans have, and they'll almost certainly be here long after our species is gone.

Entomologists—biologists who specialize in entomology, the study of insects—have identified almost ten thousand different species of ants. But that may be only a small part of the total. Dr. Wilson once identified forty-three different species of ants living in just one rain forest tree. He thinks there may be 10,000, 20,000, or even 30,000 other ant species yet to be discovered. Because they are little noticed by most humans, very few ants have common names. And those few common names—such as harvester ant, fire ant, or carpenter ant—often refer to a group of similar kinds of ants rather than one individual species.

Ants in Story and Folklore

People have coexisted with ants for all of human history. So it's not surprising they appear in folklore, stories, and myths. In Greek mythology, a young girl named Myrmex was a favorite of the goddess Athena. Myrmex said she invented the plow, although it was actually a gift from the goddess. To punish her, Athena turned Myrmex into an ant.

Another Greek legend describes the Myrmidons, the soldiers of Achilles. They were ants that had been transformed into an army. The English word *myrmidon* is derived from this legend. It means a soldier who carries out orders ruthlessly, without any concern for human feeling. The Greek language is also the source of the name for scientists who study ants—myrmecologists.

Around the world, people see ants busily building nests,

ANTS HAVE THE MOST SPECIES OF ANY ANIMAL ON EARTH. ALMOST 10,000 SPECIES HAVE BEEN IDENTIFIED. HERE ARE A FEW EXAMPLES OF THEIR TREMENDOUS VARIETY, IDENTIFIED BY COMMON NAMES.

Red ant

Red carpenter ant

Trap-jaw ant

Long-legged ant

Panamanian ant

carrying bits of food, and caring for their young. So in proverbs and folktales, ants are most often used to show the value of hard work. For example, an Arabic proverb reminds people to "be like the ant in the days of summer." In the Bible's book of Proverbs, King Solomon urges his people to take a lesson from the ant: "Go to the ant, thou sluggard; consider her ways and be wise." In *Poor Richard's Almanack*, Benjamin Franklin wrote "None preaches better than the ant, and she says nothing." Mark Twain noted, "As a thinker and planner the ant is the equal of any savage race of men . . . and in one or two high mental qualities she is above the reach of any man, savage or civilized."

PEOPLE ADMIRE ANTS FOR THEIR HARD WORK. THIS ONE IS CARRYING A STICK, MATERIAL FOR A NEST.

Of course, most of us know Aesop's fable of the ant and the grasshopper: Winter is approaching. A starving grasshopper begs a busy ant to share some food. "What did you do all summer?"

A 1906 FRENCH VERSION OF "THE ANT AND THE GRASSHOPPER" APPEARS IN *THE FABLES OF FONTAINE*.

ANT PROVERBS

On the other hand, human activity is sometimes compared negatively to that of ants, as being endless, mindless busywork. For example, the bustle of a city or a large corporation is occasionally compared to the ceaseless activity of an anthill.

Ant anatomy is also the subject of folktales. A Korean story explains why ants have a petiole, or narrow "waist," this way: An earthworm wanted to get married, so he asked an ant to be a matchmaker. The ant arranged for a millipede to be the earthworm's wife. "Oh, no," the earthworm cried when the ant told him. "I could never afford to buy her shoes!" When the ant heard this, she laughed and went to tell the millipede. "Oh, well," the millipede said. "The earthworm is so long, I'd never be able to make enough clothes for him." The ant thought this was extremely funny. She laughed so hard she thought her stomach might burst, so she tied a rope around her waist. To this day, all ants have a tiny waist.

Ants are also thought to foretell the weather, or personal fortune. In some parts of the world, including the United States, people say that stepping on ants will bring rain. Ants busily carrying what people think are their eggs, but are actually pupae, to safety from a disturbed nest are considered a sign of a coming storm.

In some cultures killing ants is thought to bring bad luck. In India and other parts of the world, an ant nest in a home or the bite of an ant are said to bring good fortune or wealth. In Mexican folklore, however, ants in the house are a sign that someone is trying to send the family bad luck.

Ants are also part of various folk customs. In Finland, for example, boys are told to eat ants in the spring to help them grow up strong. An Arabian custom has parents put an ant in the hand of a newborn son, saying, "May the boy turn out clever and skillful." In South America, Arawak mothers allow an ant to bite their toddlers, believing this will help the children learn to walk. Young Arawak men and women must also withstand painful ant bites before they can marry.

ANTS ARE THE SUBJECT OF FOLKLORE AND PROVERBS THROUGHOUT THE WORLD. ENDLESSLY INDUSTRIOUS AND LINKED BY COMPLEX SOCIAL RELATIONSHIPS—IT'S NO WONDER PEOPLE INVEST THESE TINY CREATURES WITH MEANING.

the ant asks. "I spent the summer making music," the grasshopper answers. Of course, the ant spent *her* summer gathering food for the coming winter. She refuses to share her harvest. "Since you spent all summer singing," the ant says coldly, "you'll have to spend the winter dancing."

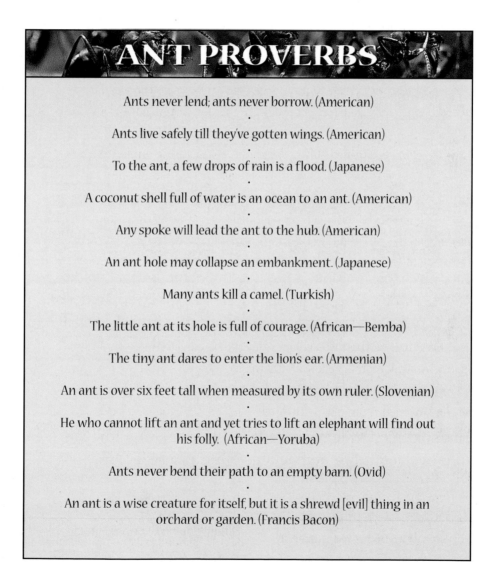

ANT PROVERBS

Ants never lend; ants never borrow. (American)

·

Ants live safely till they've gotten wings. (American)

·

To the ant, a few drops of rain is a flood. (Japanese)

·

A coconut shell full of water is an ocean to an ant. (American)

·

Any spoke will lead the ant to the hub. (American)

·

An ant hole may collapse an embankment. (Japanese)

·

Many ants kill a camel. (Turkish)

·

The little ant at its hole is full of courage. (African—Bemba)

·

The tiny ant dares to enter the lion's ear. (Armenian)

·

An ant is over six feet tall when measured by its own ruler. (Slovenian)

·

He who cannot lift an ant and yet tries to lift an elephant will find out his folly. (African—Yoruba)

·

Ants never bend their path to an empty barn. (Ovid)

·

An ant is a wise creature for itself, but it is a shrewd [evil] thing in an orchard or garden. (Francis Bacon)

2 Ant Evolution

Aforaging ant climbs up the trunk of a tree. Her antennae wave back and forth, seeking the scents that might mean food is nearby. But as she climbs across the bark, one foot steps in a drop of sticky sap. She is trapped. The sap holds the ant in place. More sap oozes from the tree, and soon she is entombed. The sap slowly crystallizes around her.

Eventually, the tree falls and is covered with earth. Twenty-five million years later, a human fossil hunter finds the chunk of sap. Over the centuries it has hardened into a clear, golden gem called amber. Trapped deep within the honey-colored stone is the ancient ant—an ant almost identical to its living relatives in the twenty-first century.

Early Ants

How did modern-day ants evolve? Figuring out how any creature evolved is like putting together a complex jigsaw puzzle—

ANCIENT ANTS HAVE BEEN FOSSILIZED IN AMBER.

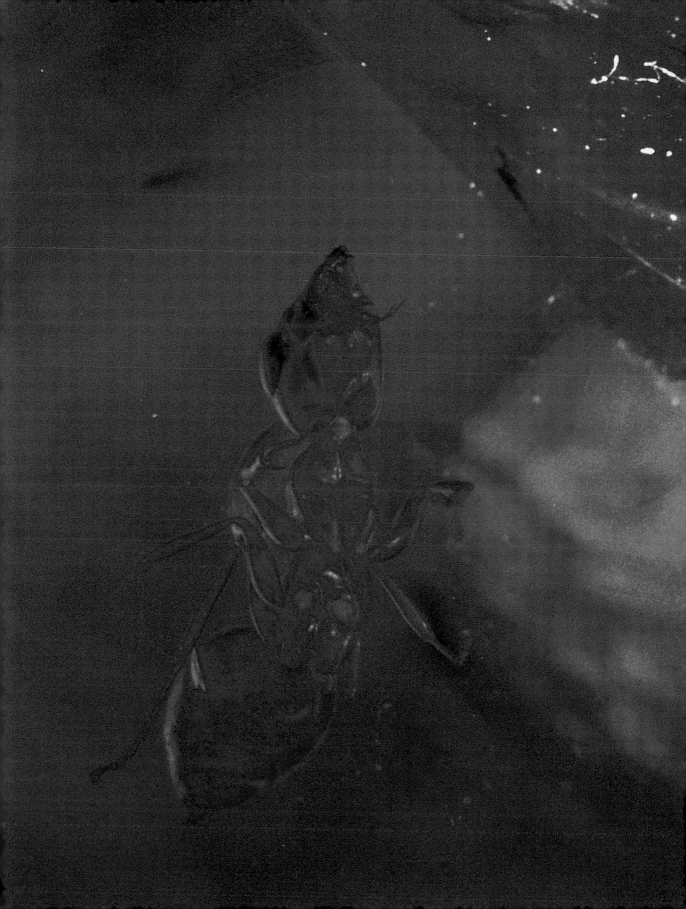

without a picture to guide you and with many of the pieces missing. In the end, you have to make logical conclusions about what the finished puzzle looks like without being certain you have it exactly right.

The best information about evolution comes from fossils. Fossils form when an animal or plant dies and is covered with layers of mud or other sediment. Over many centuries, the sediment hardens and turns to stone. Hidden in that stone is the imprint of the long-dead creature.

Unfortunately, the fossil record of insects is not very detailed. Because they are small and don't have hard, bony skeletons, insects don't preserve well as fossils. We know much more about ancient fish and reptiles than we do about early insects. Nevertheless, a few stony fossils of early ants and their ancestors do exist.

Other clues about ant evolution are found fossilized in amber and in the physical features of closely related modern animals such as wasps. This evidence is enough to allow myrmecologists to piece together the early history of the ant family.

Ants and all other insects belong to a large group of animals called arthropods. Arthropod means "jointed leg." All arthropods have hard exoskeletons (outer coverings); bodies divided into segments, or sections; and legs that can bend and move at several different joints. The earliest arthropod fossils are found in rocks dating from about 500 million years ago. The first insects probably evolved about 390 million years ago.

Ants belong to an order of insects called Hymenoptera—a group that also includes bees and wasps. About 200 million years ago the first Hymenopterans appeared. And somewhere between 100 and 120 million years ago, the first ants evolved. By contrast, our species, *Homo sapiens*, has existed on Earth for less than a million years.

Ant evolution

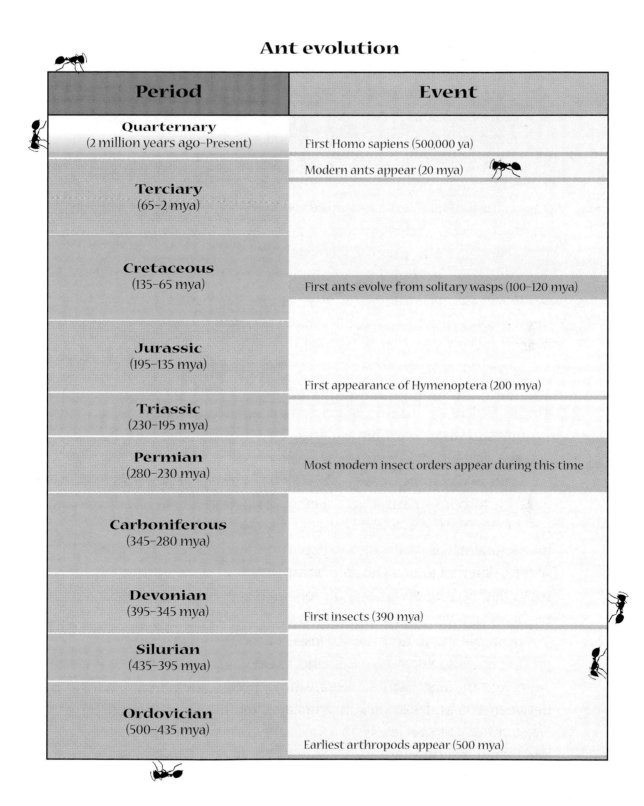

Period	Event
Quarternary (2 million years ago–Present)	First Homo sapiens (500,000 ya)
Terciary (65–2 mya)	Modern ants appear (20 mya)
Cretaceous (135–65 mya)	First ants evolve from solitary wasps (100–120 mya)
Jurassic (195–135 mya)	First appearance of Hymenoptera (200 mya)
Triassic (230–195 mya)	
Permian (280–230 mya)	Most modern insect orders appear during this time
Carboniferous (345–280 mya)	
Devonian (395–345 mya)	First insects (390 mya)
Silurian (435–395 mya)	
Ordovician (500–435 mya)	Earliest arthropods appear (500 mya)

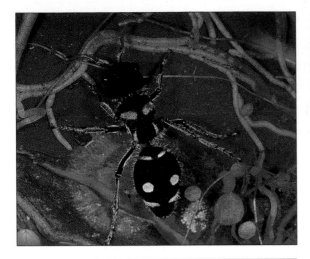

WASPS AND ANTS ARE CLOSELY RELATED. THIS "VELVET ANT" IS ACTUALLY A WINGLESS WASP.

BY LOOKING AT THIS PAPER WASP, IT'S EASY TO SEE MANY SIMILARITIES BETWEEN ANTS AND WASPS.

To picture how much longer ants have been on Earth than humans have, imagine yourself standing beside the Empire State Building. Let your height represent the length of time human beings have existed. The height of the Empire State Building then represents the time ants have existed.

Scientists think the earliest ants evolved from solitary wasps—wasps that hunted and reproduced as individuals, rather than living in colonies. In fact, modern-day wasps and ants are still very similar in appearance. The earliest ant fossils have such wasplike features as short jaws with only two teeth. However, they also show many characteristics of modern ants, such as antennae with a long first segment.

Over 50 to 60 million years, ants gradually evolved into many different species. (A species is one particular type of organism that is able to reproduce more of its own kind.) They adapted to many different habitats and food opportunities and developed more complex social behavior. By 50 million years ago, ants had spread across the globe in huge numbers. They had become one of the dominant creatures on Earth.

By 20 million years ago, ants had evolved into forms we would recognize today. Fossil ants from that distant time are nearly identical in appearance to modern ants. They are so similar that a twenty-first-century myrmecologist can examine a 20-million-year-old ant entombed within a piece of polished amber and identify its species.

The Roots of Social Behavior

Evolution occurs over vast periods of time, as individual organisms pass their genes from generation to generation. Individuals of any species vary slightly from one to another. Some variations—such as a better sense of smell or a tendency to spend more energy caring for young—may increase that organism's chance of surviving and reproducing. When that individual reproduces, the helpful variation is passed to the next generation. Gradually, as those changes spread through more and more individuals, the species evolves into something new.

The fact that ants have survived for so long with so little change shows how successfully they have adapted. In particular, their social behavior gives them a tremendous advantage. In most animals, a single adult raises the young. And when one adult is responsible for all the needs of its young, failure at just one task brings death to the offspring.

However, each new generation of ants is raised by an entire colony of workers. All the workers in a colony are sisters. And the workers specialize in different tasks. Some hunt while others dig; some care for developing larvae while others defend the colony against predators. This division of labor is much more

ANTS IN THE COLONY WORK TOGETHER TO FEED AND CARE FOR THE YOUNG.

efficient than a single adult trying to accomplish everything on its own. When one worker dies or fails at a task, life in the colony goes on.

Here's how biologists think the social behavior of ants may have come about: Ants evolved from solitary wasps that stung and paralyzed their prey—a caterpillar, for example—and then laid their eggs on it. The larvae fed on the captured prey as they developed. Later in the evolutionary development of wasps, the females began building nests to protect their larvae. Even further along, the females stayed with the larvae, feeding and caring for them as they grew. In the next step, long-lived females survived until their larvae matured. Daughters stayed with their mother, rearing young of their own. Or perhaps groups of sister offspring remained in a single nest, raising their young together.

Over many thousand of generations, the females' behavior became more and more antlike. They began to cooperate in gathering and sharing food. After that, divisions of labor gradually formed. One female—the queen—produced the eggs while the others gathered food and cared for the young. Eventually the colony developed the ability to produce either queens or workers by feeding and caring for larvae differently.

Remember, these events took place very gradually, over many millions of years. Insects reproduce quickly and their life spans are short. Wasps and ants produce at least one new generation each year. So the changes that created ant society evolved over millions of generations.

Ant altruism

Ant workers gather food and then pass it on to other members of the colony. They dig chambers for other ants to use. They even sacrifice their lives to defend their colony. The workers' efforts enable the queen to produce a brood of reproductive males and females, brothers and sisters that will fly away to start new colonies. The willingness of individual ants to sacrifice for the benefit of the colony is known as altruism.

It's easy to see why living in a colony is an advantage for a queen. Social living makes it much more likely that her offspring will survive and reproduce. But what advantages do *workers* get

EXAMPLES OF ALTRUISM: (ABOVE) ANTS PROTECT LARVAE FROM A LADYBUG.
(BELOW) AN ANT REMOVES A DEAD WORKER FROM THE NEST.

by cooperating? How does altruism help *them* pass their genes to the next generation? It is almost always the queen that produces the next generation of offspring. So how do workers evolve genes for cooperative behavior? These are some of the most interesting questions in evolutionary biology.

The key to these puzzles lies in the way ants reproduce. Ants, bees, and wasps inherit their genes through a process called haplodiploidy. This term simply means that fertilized eggs always become female and unfertilized eggs become male.

Queens mate early in their lives. They store millions of sperm from their mating flight in a reservoir called the spermatheca. When a queen fertilizes her eggs with the sperm, the eggs develop into females, either workers or new queens. These female offspring are diploid—meaning they have two sets of genes, one from their mother and one from their father. When the queen releases unfertilized eggs, they develop into males. Males are haploid—they have only one set of genes.

A LEAFCUTTER ANT QUEEN IS MUCH LARGER THAN THE WORKERS OF THE COLONY.

Haplodiploidy has a surprising result. Workers are more closely related to one another than they are to their mother! When animals reproduce, they ordinarily get a mixture of genes, half from their mother and half from their father. Brothers and sisters of most species share about half their genes with each other and, of course, with each parent.

But unlike most other animals, male ants have only one set of genes—their mother's. So when the queen ant passes her mate's genes on to her daughters, each set is exactly the same. Sister workers in the colony share as much as three-quarters of their genes with one another—half of their mother's genes and all of their father's.

What does this mean for evolution? It means that a worker's best strategy for passing her genes on to the next generation is to help some of her sisters have offspring. And although they look very different from the workers, new queens raised by the colony are also their sisters. Helping the new queens survive and reproduce gives each worker the best chance of passing her own genes on to future generations. The workers do this by caring for the larvae, gathering food, and, if necessary, giving up their own lives to protect the colony. The workers seem altruistic. But in fact, they are selfishly doing their best to reproduce—through their sisters' survival.

How do males fit into the colony's reproductive plan? Males come from unfertilized eggs. They have half their mother's genes and no father at all. So they share only one-quarter of their genes with their sisters. Of course, some males are needed to mate with new queens. But it is in the ants' best interest to invest as little energy as possible in these nonworking, more distantly related members of the colony. So colonies produce short-lived males just once a year, in numbers just large enough to ensure the fertilization of new queens.

How are ants related to other creatures? Biologists classify each kind of organism to show how it is related to the millions of other living things. Each species is grouped with similar species in a genus (plural, genera), based on characteristics that they share. Closely related genera are then grouped into families, and so on.

There are more than 9,500 known species of ants. Biologists place all ant species within a single family, Formicidae. Here are the groups and subgroups that scientists currently use to classify ants among the other members of the animal kingdom.

Kingdom: Animalia—all animals

Phylum: Arthropoda—animals with jointed legs, a hard exoskeleton, and segmented bodies.

Class: Insecta—arthropods with three body sections (head, thorax, and abdomen); three pairs of legs and one pair of antennae; usually two pairs of wings.

Order: Hymenoptera (sawflies, ants, wasps, and bees)— Insects with two pairs of membranous wings; clubbed, segmented antennae; and chewing, or chewing and sucking, mouthparts.

Suborder: Apocrita—abdomen and thorax separated by a petiole ("waist"); ovipositor (egg-laying tube) adapted for piercing or stinging; many with social organization; many carnivorous (feed on other animals); larvae usually legless.

Superfamily: Scolioidea—ants and parasitic wasps.

Family: Formicidae—the ant family, including more than 9,500 species, perhaps 10,000–30,000 additional species yet to be identified.

3 The Ant, Inside and Out

A foraging wood ant finds a dead moth in the leaf litter beneath a tree. She examines it carefully with her antennae. The moth is ten times the ant's weight, but that doesn't stop her. She grasps it firmly in her jaws and lifts it easily into the air. Then she quickly scurries down the trail on her six jointed legs. She carries her find to the colony's nest, moving almost as fast as if she had no load at all.

Ants accomplish surprising feats of strength and power. Workers can pick up and carry loads that are ten, twenty, or even fifty times their own weight. And they hardly slow down as they carry their burdens. If an average man did an equivalent amount of work, he would be able to lift an object weighing a ton and run with it for miles at top speed.

Don't let their size fool you. Ants' bodies are remarkably complicated. Each ant has a heart and blood, muscles, a digestive system, a system of glands, sense organs, nerves, and a

THIS CENTRAL AMERICAN ANT HAS A POWERFUL STING.

brain. Believe it or not, myrmecologists have dissected many ant specimens and carefully examined their organs. Scientists know quite a lot about how these tiny creatures are put together.

The Body: Size and Structure

Ants vary widely in size. The smallest ants are only about 1/25 inch (1 mm) long. The largest ant species, while still tiny when compared with a human, are hundreds of times larger. The largest ants grow to about one inch (2.5 cm).

Within individual colonies, different castes, or groups, of ants have different body forms that enable them to carry out different tasks. The queen is the largest member of the colony and the only one that produces offspring. Some species have more than one queen per colony. The next-largest members of the colony are the males. Like young queens, the males have wings. The colony usually produces males only once a year. They do no work and die soon after mating.

The rest of the colony is made up one or more castes of workers. All workers are female. Many species have several different castes of workers. The largest, known as majors, or soldiers, defend the colony. Smaller workers, called medias, and minors—the smallest caste of workers—carry out other tasks such as foraging, housekeeping, and caring for the brood.

Ants are covered with a stiff outer covering called an exoskeleton. This hard shell protects the ant's soft internal organs. Most ants' exoskeletons are black, brown, red, or yellow, although a few species are a metallic blue or green color. The exoskeleton is made of chitin, the same stiff material from which crab and shrimp shells are made. Many species have sharp spines on their exoskeletons that make them less attractive to predators.

Ants have no bones. Their muscles attach directly to the

THIS ARMY ANT SOLDIER DEFENDS THE COLONY WITH LARGE, POWERFUL JAWS.

inside of their exoskeleton. The muscles exert their power by pulling against the chitin.

Like other insects, an ant's body is divided into three sections: the head, the thorax, and the abdomen.

At the front of the ant's head are the mandibles, or jaws. Mandibles come in many different shapes and sizes, depending on the ant's species and caste. Seen from close up, mandibles are terrible weapons. They are miniature blades, pincers, or curved swords edged with sharp, pointed teeth. Mandibles are not just for cutting and fighting. They are also the ant's "hands."

Whenever a worker has to pick up a larva, move a grain of sand, or carry a piece of food, she uses her mandibles.

Behind the mandibles are another, smaller pair of jaws called maxillae. Ants use their maxillae to chew food into tiny bits before they lick it into their mouth with their tongue.

Farther back on the ant's head are a pair of antennae and a pair of compound eyes. Some species also have three small simple eyes called ocelli on the top of their heads. All ant antennae have a long segment attached to the head and several shorter segments. Ordinarily the antennae have an elbowlike bend where the short segments join the long one.

The middle section of the ant's body is called the thorax. The thorax contains most of the ant's muscles. All six legs are attached to the thorax. Each leg has nine jointed segments and two small hooks for grasping, climbing, and digging. Ants are very tidy creatures. Their two front legs are equipped with fine

THE ANT'S MANDIBLES ARE USED FOR CUTTING, FIGHTING, AND GRASPING.

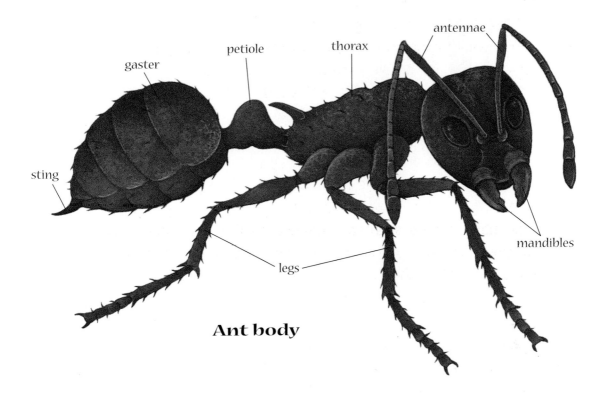

gaster | petiole | thorax | antennae

sting

mandibles

legs

Ant body

combs they use for cleaning themselves. The wings of reproductive males and females are also attached to the thorax.

The rear section of the ant is called the abdomen. It is made
up of the narrow petiole and the much larger gaster. The gaster
contains most of the ant's digestive system, as well as several
very important glands. Many ant species have a stinger at the
very end of their gaster.

Food

Many ants are carnivorous, meaning that they eat insects and
other small animals. Other species of ants eat seeds or other
parts of plants as well, which makes them omnivorous (both
meat- and plant-eating). And many ants also include plant nectar or the sweet honeydew produced by aphids and other
insects in their diets.

THIS ANT IS EATING A
BUTTERFLY EGG.

Ants can swallow only liquid food. An ant chews her food
into a paste with her maxillae. She uses her tongue to move the
paste into a small pouch in her mouth. Muscles in the pouch
squeeze the paste, and the ant swallows the liquid. Then the ant
spits out the dry pellet. The pellets—sometimes called castings—
are dropped onto the colony's midden, or waste pile.

The liquid food travels through the ant's esophagus, a long
tube that runs from the head, through the thorax and petiole,
and into the gaster. In the gaster, each ant has a crop, or social
stomach. Ants store liquid food in their crop to share with nestmates. A hungry ant asks for food by touching her sister's
mouthparts. The ant with food then regurgitates (spits up) a
droplet to feed her nestmate.

Food passes from the crop to the rest of the digestive system—the "true" stomach and intestine, where nutrients are absorbed into the blood. Digestive wastes are expelled from the rectum as liquid feces.

Oxygen

Like any other animal, ants need oxygen. But ants' bodies are so small that they don't need lungs or gills to absorb it into their bloodstream. Instead, they get oxygen directly from the air. Tiny openings, called spiracles, allow air to pass through the exoskeleton and into the body. The ant's blood absorbs the oxygen and carries it to all the cells. Waste carbon dioxide is released into the air through the spiracles in the same way.

An ant's blood is clear, not red like our own. Neither do ants have blood vessels. Instead, they have a simple heart and

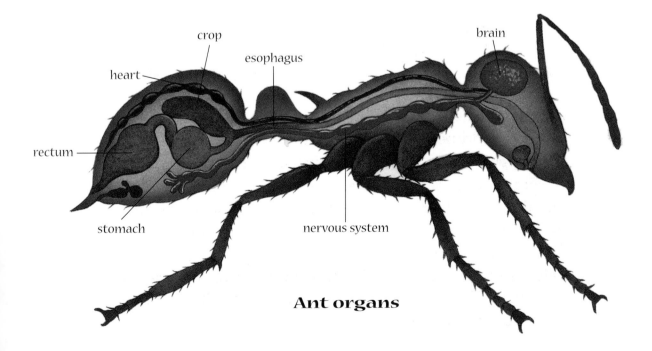

Ant organs

open circulatory system. The heart is a long muscular tube that extends from the head to the gaster. Blood enters the heart in the gaster. The heart pumps it toward the ant's head. From there, the blood flows back through the body. It bathes all the organs, bringing nutrients and oxygen to every cell, and carrying away wastes.

Nerves and Senses

The brain of an ant is tiny, of course. But it's quite large for an animal of its size. Messages from the brain travel to and from the rest of the body through a nerve cord. This cord extends from the brain to the gaster. It is located in the ventral, or "belly," side of the ant, below the esophagus. Along the nerve cord is a series of ganglia—bundles of nerves connected to the ant's muscles and sense organs. The ganglia relay nerve signals to and from the brain.

The ant's main sense organs are its antennae. Antennae receive both touch and chemical (smell) information. An ant's antennae are in almost constant motion, as the ant examines its environment.

In addition to antennae, most ants are covered with microscopic touch-sensitive hairs. Ants also have nerves in their tongue to provide a sense of taste. Though ants do not have ears, they "hear" with chordotonal organs that sense vibrations. These organs are found on their antennae, legs, trunk, and head.

Ants see with compound eyes, one on each side of the head. Each eye is made of many individual light-sensitive facets. Winged males and females have the most highly developed eyes, enabling them to see clearly enough to find one another in flight. Ants also navigate by tracking the position of the sun. In addition to their compound eyes, many species also sense

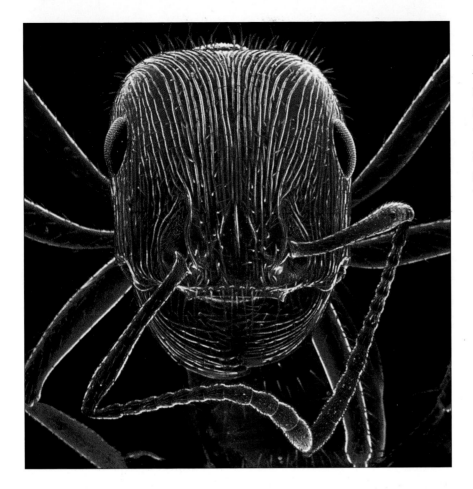

light and dark with three smaller ocelli on the top of their head. Ocelli are very sensitive to low levels of light. They may help ants orient themselves in the dim light that filters into their nests.

Experiments show that ants see well enough to use visual landmarks such as stones or plants to guide them as they forage. And they are intelligent enough to learn new routes when those landmarks have moved. However, even though ants show signs of simple intelligence and problem-solving, most of their behavior is instinctive. This means they respond to stimuli in predictable ways. For example, when a larva signals that it needs food, they feed it. When an intruder enters the colony, they attack it. No "thinking" or decision-making is involved.

Glands

Ants communicate by chemical messages that they receive through their antennae. The chemicals, called pheromones, are produced within a complex system of exocrine glands.

One of these is the Dufour's gland, located in the gaster. Most ants use the pheromones from this gland to mark trails and recruit nestmates to help with a tasks. How powerful is the pheromone? Dr. Wilson estimates that 35 millionths of an ounce (1 mg) is enough to lead a trail of ants around the world three times!

In addition, ants have several other glands in the gaster, three or four more in the head, and others in the thorax. Each produces a different chemical message. For example, a pheromone from one gland in the head alerts the colony to danger. A chemical from another means "feed me." Each ant species uses a different set of pheromones as signals, and each chemical carries its own unique meaning.

ALL ANTS, INCLUDING THESE WEAVER ANTS, COMMUNICATE WITH CHEMICAL MESSAGES.

A poison gland is located in the rear of the gaster. It produces toxic chemicals that the ant injects into its enemies with her stinger. Species that don't have a stinger make formic acid in their poison gland. The ants spray this chemical from the rear of their gaster as a defense.

Reproduction

All worker ants are female. Their reproductive organs, located in the gaster, are almost always small and inactive. Workers occasionally produce an unfertilized egg that develops into a male, but ordinarily they are sterile. The only female with a working reproductive system is the queen. Because egg production takes lots of energy and nutrients, the queen is larger than the other ants.

In some species, queens produce hundreds or even thousands of eggs a day. In others, egg production is much slower. As you might expect, ovaries—the egg-producing organs—take up much of the queen's gaster. The gaster also contains her spermatheca—a reservoir to store the sperm from her mating flight. Sperm can live for many years within the spermatheca. As each egg passes through the queen's reproductive canal, she can fertilize it by releasing sperm. She then deposits the eggs through a tubular organ at the rear of her abdomen, called an ovipositor. Fertilized eggs develop into females. The queen can also release unfertilized eggs, which develop into males.

Males, or drones, have large testes—sperm-producing organs that fill much of their gasters. Males also have special clasping organs at the ends of their gasters that enable them to grasp a female and transfer sperm to her spermatheca when they mate.

4 Life Cycle

As you stroll through a wooded park on a warm summer afternoon, a silvery flash of movement on the ground catches your eye. Among the pine needles and tufts of grass is a small mound of sand and earth. Dozens of winged ants are emerging from the center of the mound, along with many smaller, wingless workers. Other winged ants swarm around the outside of the nest, crawling over the fallen leaves or climbing up grass stems. The winged ants—called alates—are the reproductive males and females of the colony. They rise into the air, guided by the faint odor of pheromones released by alates from other nearby colonies. Birds dart overhead, feasting on the bountiful, energy-rich food. Only a few of the winged ants will survive to mate and begin a new colony.

The Mating Flight

Maybe you've been lucky enough to find a colony of ants at the moment when it releases its reproductive males and females to

A WINGED ANT, OR ALATE, PREPARES TO TAKE FLIGHT.

A SWARM OF ALATES EMERGES FROM A NEST IN A WOODEN SIGN.

the skies. If so, you've seen the beginning of the ants' life cycle.

Ants are social insects. A single ant cannot survive long on its own. So when we talk about the ant's life cycle, we have to consider the life cycle of an entire colony. Scientists often speak of an ant colony as a superorganism. Although it is made of many individuals, the colony acts like a single living thing. It is the colony—not any one ant—that feeds, grows, and reproduces.

A mature ant colony usually produces sexually reproducing winged alates once a year, whenever the climate is favorable and there is plenty of food. The workers in each colony care for the alates for days or weeks. Then, when the weather is perfect, they allow them to leave the nest and take off for their nuptial (marriage) flight.

Alates from many colonies emerge at the same time. They

WORKERS ACCOMPANY THE ALATES AND URGE THEM INTO THE AIR.

release pheromones into the air to attract each another. The alates gather in clouds around bushes, treetops, or tall man-made structures. Males and females mate in the air or on a leaf or branch. In desert regions, they may simply cluster and mate on a patch of dry ground. A female often mates with several different males. She will never mate again. The new queen stores the millions of sperm in her spermatheca.

After the nuptial flight, the males die quickly. Their part in the creation of a new colony is over. The fertilized female searches for a likely spot to start her new colony. Her choice depends on her species. She lands and quickly breaks off her wings. She will never need to fly again, and wings will get in the way as she builds her nest. To remove them, she bites at them or rubs against a piece of wood or stone.

Starting a New Colony

Let's observe a ground-dwelling harvester ant queen. After mating, the young queen digs a small chamber in a patch of earth softened by a recent rain. This little enclosed room in the earth is called the claustral cell. She crawls inside the chamber, seals the entrance hole, and begins laying her first brood of eggs.

She fertilizes each egg with sperm from her spermatheca, so they will all become female workers. Only after several years, when the colony is well established, will the queen lay some eggs without releasing any sperm. Those eggs will develop into reproductive males.

The new queen doesn't eat for many weeks or months. Gradually shrinking wing muscles and stores of body fat provide the energy she needs. She also eats many of her own eggs to survive.

Metamorphosis

Like most insects, ants go through four life stages: egg, larva, pupa, and adult. This process is called complete metamorphosis. It is one of the most amazing transformations in nature. Ants begin as tiny eggs, sometimes too small to be seen with the unaided eye. After a few days, the eggs hatch into white worm-like larvae, or grubs. The whitish grubs cannot move or feed themselves. Over the next several weeks, the workers feed the larvae. All the larvae do is eat and grow. Ant larvae consume much more food than adult ants do.

Once the larvae have finished growing they pupate. A pupa is a resting stage, during which the larvae metamorphose (change) into their adult form. Many insects, including some species of ants, pupate within a silky cocoon that they spin around themselves. Other ant species pupate without a cocoon. Instead, they metamorphose inside a papery translucent skin. If you've ever found an ant colony under a stone or a rotting log, you've probably seen the workers scurrying back and forth, carrying the helpless pupae to safety. People often mistake these pupae for the ants' eggs.

The pupae change, gradually and completely. They then emerge from their cocoons or skins as adult ants. The newly

WORKERS FEED AND CARE FOR THE LARVAE THAT HAVE HATCHED FROM THE QUEEN'S EGGS.

WHEN THE PUPAE ARE READY TO EMERGE, WORKERS HELP BY CHEWING THROUGH THE COCOONS OR SKINS.

emerged workers are known as callows. At first, they are light colored, soft-bodied, and weak. Over a few days, their exoskeletons harden. The ants darken, gain strength, and take their places as full adult members of the colony.

Different species of ants go through the various stages of metamorphosis at different rates. The entire process may take a few weeks or as much as a couple of months.

The Growth of a Colony

Let's return to the new queen in her underground chamber. She feeds the growing larvae of her first brood unfertilized alimentary (food) eggs and nutrient-rich saliva. During this early phase of a new colony's life, only about ten to twenty percent of the eggs develop into adults. The rest are used for food. Workers in a young queen's first brood are smaller than normal and shorter-lived as well. This is because they haven't been fed the same complete diet that larvae in a mature nest receive.

When they emerge from their pupal stage, the new workers dig their way out of the claustral chamber and start foraging for food. Meanwhile the queen lays more eggs. The new workers begin feeding the queen and caring for the eggs and larvae.

AN ADULT LEAFCUTTER ANT TENDS A BROOD OF EGGS, LARVAE, AND PUPAL.

A RED ANTS' NEST AND A COLONY OF IMPORTED FIRE ANTS HAVE BEEN SLICED OPEN TO SHOW THE PASSAGES WITHIN THE MOUNDS.

island of Hokkaido, Japan. This colony of *Formica yessensis* ants lived in 45,000 connected nests, spread across almost 700 acres (280 ha). This supercolony probably contained over 300 million workers and more than a million queens!

EXPERIMENT WITH ANTS

nts make excellent experimental subjects for science fair projects or other investigations. Here are some ideas for experiments you might want to try:

How do ants react to an obstacle in their path? Place a standard obstacle (such as a block of wood) in the path of a line of ants. Time how long it takes for the ants to find their way around the obstacle and resume their normal gathering. Observe and record their behavior as they solve the problem.

A GROUP OF TROPICAL ANTS GATHERS AROUND A DROP OF SUGAR WATER.

How quickly will ants find a food source? Place a piece of food at a standard distance, such as one yard (1 m), from an ant colony. Time how long it takes them to find it and begin feeding. You might experiment to see if they find some foods more quickly than others, or if some species of ants seem to find the food more quickly than others.

How do ants relocate a food source if their trail is moved? Place a food source on the center of a piece of paper or cardboard, near an ant colony. Allow the ants to start feeding. Then carefully brush the ants off the paper. Turn the paper 90 degrees. Observe to see if and how they relocate the food or their trail.

What foods do ants prefer? Weigh out small, equal amounts of different foods (such as sugar, crushed cornflakes, small pieces of cooked hamburger meat, or bits of vegetables). Place the foods near an ant colony. After the ants have had the opportunity to find the food and feed for a specified time, count the number of foraging visits to each kind of food to see which the ants seem to be most attracted to.

Which common household substances form an effective ant barrier? Find an ant trail, or establish one by placing some food on a sidewalk. Then lay a thin strip of a common household substance (such as baking soda, salt, detergent, or borax) across the trail. Observe which substances serve as a barrier to the ants' foraging, and which do not.

5 Life in an Ant Colony

A young colony of red harvester ants has built a sandy mound in the Arizona desert. Workers scurry in and out of opening in the center. Some carry out grains of sand that they deposit on the edge of the mound. A few ants follow a trail away from the nest. Others return carrying seeds or other bits of food. Each time two workers meet they pause briefly to touch antennae. But what is happening deep underground, in the rest of the colony? How do these tiny creatures spend their days?

Communication

Ants don't see very well, and much of their time is spent in the dark anyway. So ant communication depends mainly on touch, taste, and smell. As the ants touch one another and share food, chemical signals quickly pass through the colony. How fast and

CARPENTER ANTS DON'T EAT WOOD, BUT THEY BUILD THEIR NESTS IN IT.

AN ENTRANCE TO AN ANT COLONY IN TROPICAL VENEZUELA.

efficient is this communication system? Just disturb an anthill with a stick and see how quickly the ants come pouring out to defend their home.

Each colony seems to have its own "nest smell," which allows ants to recognize nestmates and identify intruders. Scientists are not sure where this unique odor comes from. They suspect it may originate from the material used in building a particular nest or from substances the queen produces that are passed to all members of the colony.

When two ants meet, they touch each other with their antennae, their organs of smell. If they recognize one another as nestmates, they quickly move on. But any outsider—even a member of the same species—is in danger. Away from the nest, foraging ants often ignore a "foreign" ant. But when outsiders come too close to the nest or try to enter the colony, they will usually be thrown out or killed.

TWO ANTS MEET AND TOUCH EACH OTHER WITH THEIR ANTENNAE.

ANTS SHARE WHATEVER THEY HAVE. HERE, A WORKER SHARES A DROP OF WATER WITH ONE OF HER NESTMATES.

Each chemical from an ant's glands communicates a different message to other members of the colony. For example, foraging ants use one chemical message to mark a trail to a food source. Another chemical, sometimes combined with certain touches and movements, recruits more ants to help with a task. Yet another spreads an alarm throughout the colony. The queen and the larvae also produce chemical signals when they need attention from the workers.

Ants can send between ten and twenty different chemical messages. And each species has its own unique set of signals. A chemical that means "follow me" to one species might mean nothing to another or might carry a completely different meaning such as "alarm." Different castes of ants also produce characteristic chemicals, so a colony "knows" if it has enough soldiers or queen larvae based on the amount of special chemicals circulating among the workers.

Ants also communicate using sound vibrations called stridulations. Ants stridulate to call for assistance. To make this call, ants rub a ridged section on their abdomen with a scraper on their petiole. This produces a squeaking sound that humans can just barely hear. Ants don't have ears; they pick up the vibrations with chordotonal organs—sense organs in their antennae, legs, trunk, and head. Carpenter ants and others that live in solid nests may also warn each other of danger by tapping their heads on the nesting material.

Food Gathering

Ants have evolved to take advantage of a wide variety of foods. Most ants prey on other small invertebrates. Many also drink plant nectar and gather honeydew—a sweet excretion from aphids and other insects. Other ants harvest seeds or fruit.

Some ant species, such as leafcutter ants, forage twenty-four hours a day. Others only gather food at certain times. For example, harvester ants of the southwestern United States gather seeds in the cool morning hours, rest during the hottest part of the day, and may return to foraging in the late afternoon.

For most species, foraging begins with scout ants. Scouts usually follow main trails away from the colony and then branch out to search for food. When a scout finds something edible, she lays down a fresh trail of pheromones back to the main trail or to the colony itself. Then, using chemical messages and touches, the scout recruits more foragers to return to the food source and harvest it for the colony.

You've probably been taught to share your food with friends and siblings. But you wouldn't want to share the way ants do. Ants store and carry liquid food in their crop. A hungry ant asks for food by touching another worker's mouthparts. If that worker has food in her crop, she regurgitates some for her hungry sister. This

THESE ANTS ARE CARRYING A CAPTURED CATERPILLAR TO THEIR NEST.

ANTS PRACTICE TROPHALLAXIS: THEY FEED EACH OTHER BY REGURGITATING LIQUID FOOD FROM THEIR CROP, OR "SOCIAL STOMACH."

behavior is called trophallaxis. Through trophallaxis, food gets distributed throughout the colony.

Only a small percentage of adult workers serve as foragers. Foraging seems to be a job for the colony's oldest workers. It is hard and dangerous work. Foragers face harsh weather, predators, and conflicts with other ants. A study of one species found that foragers only survived for about fourteen days. Scientists investigating another species found its foragers survived for an average of only six days. But during that time each forager brought fifteen to twenty times its own weight in food back to the nest.

Serving the Queen

The queen produces chemicals that are very attractive to the workers. They lick her and touch her and later spread these substances throughout the colony. The workers also supply the queen with plenty of food so that she can continue producing eggs.

After the queen has laid her eggs, workers gather them and carry them to brood chambers in the nest. Most species stack the eggs neatly. Workers move the eggs, larvae, and pupae to various parts of the nest—sometimes several times a day—so that they receive the right amount of warmth and moisture.

Since larvae also produce substances that are attractive to workers, they are licked, touched, and fed generously. Workers

ONE OF THE WORKERS' MANY JOBS IS TO CARE FOR THE DEVELOPING LARVAE AND PUPAE.

chew insect parts or other food into a pulp before feeding it to the larvae. They also feed larvae by trophallaxis and with secretions from a gland in their head. Growing larvae consume much of the food foragers collect. Some research suggests that larvae help the colony digest solid food, returning some of it to the adults in the liquid form they need. When the pupae finish their metamorphosis, the workers help release the new adults by chewing through their cocoons or papery coverings.

Construction Work

Bees and wasps always build their nests in a standard hexagonal pattern, but ants are more adaptable. No two nests look exactly alike. Ants build their nests to suit a particular location and to fill the needs of their species. For example, some kinds of ants excavate underground nests, while others make their homes in hollow tree stems or rotting wood. However, ant nests ordinarily share some features. For example, most colonies build a large chamber in the center of the nest for the queen. Other chambers are used for raising larvae or storing food. Some species also build chambers to serve as middens, or garbage dumps.

As an ant colony grows, it needs more space. Workers are constantly building new galleries (passageways) and chambers and repairing old ones. Every grain of sand or chip of rotted wood must be carried out from the nest in the mandibles of a worker. How much work do these tiny creatures do? Let's look at a leafcutter ants' nest in the American tropics as an example. The nest might be twenty feet (6 m) deep and may cover a surface area of 2,700 square feet (250 sq m). The nest sometimes has more than a thousand separate entrances. To construct it, the ants move up to forty tons of soil!

Ants control their environment as they build. For instance,

LEAFCUTTER ANTS MOVE TONS OF SOIL TO BUILD A SINGLE UNDERGROUND NEST.

leafcutter ants maintain a network of bare earthen paths that they clear of leaves, twigs, and other obstacles. They also ventilate their nests well by raising the center. Air warmed by the underground activities of the ants passes out of openings near the center of the nest. As the warm air rises, cooler fresh air is drawn into other openings at the outer edges. European wood ants use a similar ventilation system in their above-ground mounds.

Many species of ants build or line their nests with a spongy material called carton. This cardboardlike material is made of chewed wood and soil, glued together with the ants' saliva. Paper wasps and hornets build their entire nests of a similar material. But for ants, carton makes up only a part of the nest's structure, the rest is built with wood, earth, or leaves.

LEAFCUTTER WORKERS CLEAR AND MAINTAIN A SYSTEM OF PATHWAYS THROUGH THE
FOREST.

Cleanliness

Ants accomplish tremendous feats of building and harvesting. But myrmecologists have discovered that they are not as busy as we think. The typical worker spends only about one-third of her time working. The rest of her time is spent resting, grooming, or just moving around.

Ants are extremely clean creatures. They spend large amounts of time cleaning themselves and their nestmates with their tongues and the combs on their forelegs. Grooming removes dust, fungus spores, and harmful bacteria. Ants even produce antibiotic substances in a special gland that they spread over their bodies to help kill germs.

You wouldn't expect such clean animals to leave trash lying around, and they don't. Each ant colony has a special garbage

ANTS GROOM THEMSELVES TO REMOVE DUST, BACTERIA, AND FUNGI.

dump, called a midden, where they get rid of feces, food castings, and even dead nestmates. Workers carry any unwanted material to the midden and drop it on the pile. Middens are often easy to spot since they are placed near nest entrances. Some species dig separate underground chambers to serve as middens.

Warfare

The main threat to most ant colonies comes from other ants. Other than humans, ants are the only creatures on Earth that engage in organized warfare—fighting with others of their kind in large groups. Most ants defend their territory fiercely. If other ants threaten a colony's territory, workers will fight to the death. Losing a few workers does little or no harm to the colony as a whole.

Many species have a specialized caste of large soldier ants

TWO AFRICAN CARPENTER ANTS FROM RIVAL COLONIES FIGHT TO THE DEATH.

whose job is to fight. But all workers defend the colony. When an ant is attacked, it releases alarm pheromones. These chemicals recruit other colony members to join the battle.

Ants are equipped with a wide range of weapons. Their hard, spiny exoskeletons serve as armor. Sharp, toothed mandibles can chop an enemy to pieces. The jaws of many species—such as the Aztec ants of Central America—can cut human skin. Like many other species, Aztec ants produce formic acid in their poison glands. They spray the acid from their gaster as a weapon. The acid makes ant bites painful to humans; to other insects, the spray can be fatal.

Other ant species have stingers at the end of their abdomens, much like their wasp ancestors. A bee dies after it stings once, but most ants can use their stingers repeatedly. The bullet ants of the South and Central American rain forests and bulldog ants of Australia are well known for their powerful, painful stings.

Certain ant species produce pheromones that confuse or panic their opponents in battle. One variety of Asian carpenter ant even defends its colony with suicide bombers. The gasters of these ants are filled with toxic liquid. When attacked, the ants squeeze the muscles in their abdomen, burst apart, and spray their enemies with poison. The exploding worker dies, of course. But the attackers are also killed or driven away and the colony is protected.

Ants don't just defend their own colonies, however. They also go on the attack. Many ants will assault and destroy weaker colonies of their own species in order to take over more territory. Ants may also attack colonies of other species that compete for food resources. Ant wars often end with the complete destruction of the weaker colony. In their book *Journey to the Ants*, Bert Hölldobler and Edward O. Wilson write, "If ants had nuclear weapons, they would probably end the world in a week."

WORKER ANTS ATTACK A QUEEN WHO IS INVADING THEIR NEST.

ATTACKING TERMITES

Some ant species specialize in preying on termites. Termites eat only wood and other plant material, so ants are always the aggressors in these battles. Termites also have complex societies, with many interesting adaptations to defend themselves from ant attacks. Some termite soldiers have powerful biting jaws. Others spray toxic chemicals at their attackers or entangle them with sticky secretions they squirt from nozzles in their heads.

Ant and termite colonies never fight to the death. Instead, the battle continues just long enough for the ants to capture the food they need. Then they retreat, carrying their prey back to the colony.

The powerful jaws, stings, and chemical defenses of worker ants make them unattractive to many predators. But some larger animals still use ants as food. Anteaters, echidnas, pangolins, and armadillos are all equipped with digging claws to unearth ants, and long sticky tongues to lap them up. Birds, lizards, toads, frogs, and many spiders and insects also prey on ants.

The winged males and females that emerge from ant colonies are an especially rich source of protein and energy. Swarms of winged ants make an attractive feast for many predators. In parts of Asia, Africa, and South America people also use alates for food. And Native Americans have used the honeypot ants of Mexico and the southwestern United States as sweet treats for centuries.

MANY CREATURES, SUCH AS THIS COLLARED ANTEATER, FEED ON ANTS.

An ant colony can be a valuable source of food and shelter for other small animals. Even with their powerful defenses, ants have many permanent visitors. Thousands of different species of insects and other arthropods live among the ants. These creatures are known as ant guests or myrmecophiles (literally, "ant lovers").

Most of the "guests" are actually parasites or predators that either disguise their odors to avoid being attacked or are too quick for the ants to catch. For example, small beetles live among the ants. To be accepted by the colony, the beetles may take on the nest smell or mimic the ants' pheromones. Some beetles get ants to share food with them by touching their mouthparts just as a sister worker would. Others eat ant larvae, eggs, or even adult workers.

Other myrmecophiles are parasites that live on the ants themselves. Parasitic flies lay their eggs on the ants. The fly larvae slowly consume and kill the ants as they grow. Tiny mites—relatives of the spiders—cling to the ants, feeding on leftovers from the ants' foraging. Other mites suck drops of blood from joints in the ants' exoskeleton or lick waxy secretions from their bodies.

Still other myrmecophiles, such as aphids and scale insects, live among the ants in mutually beneficial relationships you will read about in the next chapter.

6 Ant Agriculture

The rain forest of Central America is lush, humid, and teeming with life. Great trees rise from the forest floor; a tangle of vines and smaller plants sprouts from every branch. Colorful toucans fly from tree to tree; howler monkeys swing through the branches in search of the tastiest leaves. Brightly colored red and blue poison-arrow frogs hop along the rotting trunk of a fallen tree, hunting for insects.

But one of the most fascinating rain forest creatures is right at your feet. Endless lines of leafcutter ants parade back and forth along well-worn trails on the forest floor. Each ant looks like it's holding a tiny green umbrella. They're carrying bits of leaves harvested from nearby trees. What are they doing with all those leaves?

Co-evolution

Close relationships between different species are called symbiotic relationships. Symbiosis means "living together." In some

LEAFCUTTER ANTS HARVEST HUGE AMOUNTS OF TROPICAL VEGETATION.

to other plants nearby. Since aphids damage crops and flowers, this ant behavior causes problems for human gardeners.

Some ant species get almost all their food from trophobionts. But most ant shepherds also include other foods in their diets. Some species even eat the aphids themselves—especially old or sick ones. African weaver ants, for example, are known to kill or remove aphids when the population of trophobionts grows too large.

Some ants keep aphids in their underground nests, where they feed on plant roots. They care for the aphids' eggs over the winter, and then put the newly hatched young back on the roots to begin feeding again in the spring. If their nest is disturbed or attacked, the ants protect the aphids just as they defend their own larvae.

The mutualism of ants and trophobionts has existed for a very long time. Researchers have found fossil ants and aphids preserved together in amber at least 50 million years old.

Ant Gardeners

Other ants have evolved to become "gardeners." These species build their nests, or ant gardens, in the branches of a tree. It's easy to spot them: They look like leafy clusters sprouting wildly in the branches of a tropical tree.

The nest itself is constructed from carton, the coarse fibrous material ants make from chewed wood glued together with saliva. The nest grows gradually as the ants collect decaying plant matter, soil, and seeds. Ant gardens can grow up to two feet (60 cm) across.

Gardening ants are attracted to seeds from a variety of specialized plants. They eat the nutrient-rich food bodies attached to the seeds. They also seem to be attracted to chemicals in the

ANTS CREATED THIS GARDEN NEST ON A TREE LIMB IN THE COSTA RICAN RAIN FOREST.

seeds that mimic ant pheromones. The seeds sprout and take root in the nest. The roots hold the nest together and the branches and leaves spread out from the nest in all directions. In addition to plants, the ants also forage for prey, and may graze aphids on the roots within the nest.

Gardening ants are most common in the tropics of Central and South America, although ant gardens also grow in tropical Asia. A number of different species create garden nests. Both plants and ants benefit from these partnerships. The plants get a secure place to grow, and wastes from the ant colony fertilize them. Ants also spread the plants' seeds to other locations in the forest. Meanwhile, the plants provide food and nectar for the ants and support the nest with their roots.

Forest Rangers

In South and Central America, Africa, and Asia, some ants have formed partnerships with specific kinds of trees. If you happen to brush against one of these "ant trees," you'll soon know it.

In Central America, a particularly aggressive kind of ant makes its nest in the soft hollow core of the cecropia tree. These ants defend their tree so fiercely that scientists named them *Azteca*, after the Aztecs, great native warriors of the region. Just a gentle touch on the tree trunk brings dozens of angry ants swarming out onto the bark. The Aztec ants defend their home against any attacker, even humans or other large mammals.

Aztec ants don't sting. Instead, they bite and then spray the wound with formic acid from their gasters. In return for the ants' protection, the tree produces food bodies—small bulbs of starchy food at the base of its leaf stems. Aztec ants depend on these food bodies for almost all their nutrition.

Acacia trees in the Americas and Africa have evolved a similar partnership with *Pseudomyrmex* ants. Certain acacias have hollow thorns where the queen builds her nest. Once the colony is established, the workers chase away or kill any other insect that approaches the plant. They attack and sting larger animals that try to eat the acacia's leaves. The ants destroy any seedling that sprouts nearby, and even remove the leaves of other plants that touch their home tree. This lets the acacia take full advantage of all the available sunlight and the moisture and nutrients in the soil.

The acacia "repays" its protectors by providing a home for the colony. It also produces two different foods. At the tips of the acacia leaflets, the plant grows tiny food bodies for the ants to eat. And at the base of the leaves, the acacia provides nectaries—small openings with sweet nectar for them to drink.

THE ACACIA TREE REWARDS ITS ANT DEFENDERS WITH SWEET LIQUID FROM SPECIAL OPENINGS, CALLED NECTARIES.

The ants and the trees both benefit from this relationship. The ants can't survive without the food and shelter that their trees provide. In return, the trees get their own private security guards. Without their ant partners, the trees can still survive, but they don't grow nearly as well.

7 More Ant Specialists

Something seems slightly out of the ordinary on this steamy morning in the Amazon rain forest. There's a slight rustling in the undergrowth. Soon we hear the buzzing of many thousands of flies, and the calls of hunting birds. Lizards, snakes, small mammals, and fast-moving insects dart away through the forest. As we move closer, we notice a faint unpleasant odor in the air. At last we can see the cause of the disturbance. A squirming black tide of ants is sweeping across the forest floor.

Army Ants

Various species of army ants are common in the moist tropics. In Africa, they are called driver ants; in the Americas, they are known as legionary ants. In either case, they are unstoppable predators that capture and devour almost any creature in their path. African driver ants have sharp mandibles that allow them to consume large animals that are unable to escape. For example, a python unable to flee after eating a large meal would be fair

A CENTRAL AMERICAN ARMY ANT SOLDIER HAS SHARP, POWERFUL JAWS.

game for a swarm of driver ants. They've even been known to kill tethered farm animals and human babies.

Eciton burchelli is the most widely known and studied legionary ant in the Americas. Like most army ants, they are diurnal—moving and hunting during the day, and resting at night. As they hunt, the colony of more than a half million ants swarms across the forest floor in a broad wave fifty feet (15 m) wide and three to six feet (1-2 m) deep. The ants move at a speed of about 65 feet (20 m) per hour.

Army ants migrate in cycles. For several weeks, they remain in one place, returning from their foraging each evening. During this time, the queen produces as many as 300,000 eggs. At the same time, pupae from the previous cycle emerge as new adults.

The colony then begins its migratory phase when the eggs hatch. The hungry larvae must be fed. Each morning workers and soldiers move out in a column that gradually spreads into a wide swarm. Wherever they pass, the rain forest is swept clean of most insects and other small creatures. Army ants sometimes form living bridges or ropes, clinging together while the rest of the colony crosses an obstacle or climbs into a tree. A column of workers and soldiers follows behind the predatory swarm, carrying the larvae and guarding the queen within a crawling mass of ants.

Unlike most ants, army ants make no permanent nest. Instead, they create a temporary nest, called a bivouac, with their own bodies each evening. As evening approaches, the colony reassembles in a protected site—perhaps in a hollow log or between the roots of a tree. The ants hook their legs together to form a living nest, with the queen and larvae protected in the center.

Numerous myrmecophiles travel with each raiding colony of army ants. Certain species of beetles dart in and feed on leftovers. A black cloud of parasitic flies hovers above the raiders, attempting to lay their eggs on the ants. Several kinds of antbirds follow the swarm, feeding on escaping insects. And butterflies follow the birds, feeding on their droppings.

Unlike most ants, *Eciton burchelli* workers are blind. They use their senses of touch and smell to navigate through the forest. Maintaining physical contact with their sisters is unusually important for these ants. If a group of them becomes separated from the rest of the swarm, they will follow one another around and around in a circle. They never move outward to scout for their sisters. Unless the rest of the colony happens to reestablish contact, the isolated ants continue circling until they die.

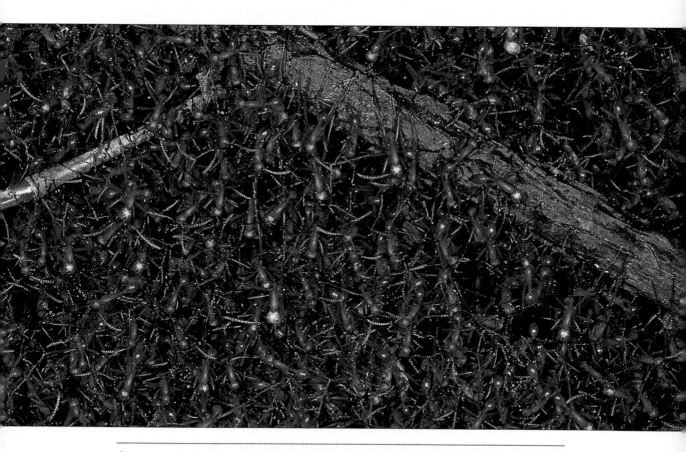

At night, army ants link their legs together to form a temporary nest, called a bivouac.

ARMY ANTS CAPTURE AND DEVOUR INSECTS AS THEY SWEEP THROUGH THE FOREST.

Eciton burchelli also reproduces in an unusual way. Males fly, but the queens don't have wings. When a colony produces a reproductive brood, some of the workers gradually become more loyal to one of the young queens. Eventually, the colony divides. Some of the workers follow the old queen. The rest travel in another direction with one of the new queens. Small groups of workers "seal off," or restrain, any other queens. They are eventually left to die. Occasionally the old queen is replaced. She too is sealed off, and both daughter colonies continue with new queens. After the colony has divided, the workers allow males from other colonies to mate with the new queens.

Weaver ants live high in the trees of tropical Africa, Asia, and Australia. More so than any other type of ant, they specialize in cooperation.

A new nest begins when a worker finds a likely leaf. She tests it. If she can bend the leaf slightly, she recruits other workers. The workers line up along the leaf and pull on the edge of the leaf together. Often they form chains. Each ant grabs another worker's petiole as they pull the edge of one leaf toward another.

Once the leaf edges have been pulled close, other workers bring larvae to the site. They too are cooperative members of the nest-building team. Each worker touches a larva to one edge of a leaf, and the larva releases a thread of sticky silk that attaches to the leaf. Then the worker moves the larva to the other leaf edge and glues the silk there. Back and forth, the workers weave the silk, holding the leaves in place. The workers seem to communicate with the larvae with taps of their antennae, telling them when to release the silk.

Other leaves are bent and glued to the growing nest. Once clustered leaves are folded and woven firmly together, they becomes a new chamber for the colony—a place to raise eggs and larvae, to protect a herd of honeydew-bearing scale insects, or for workers to rest. All the larvae's silk is used for weaving. Weaver ant larvae pupate inside the nests without cocoons.

A weaver ant colony can stretch across the tops of several neighboring trees and house a half million ants or more. Unlike most ants, weaver ants leave their droppings everywhere in their territory. The droppings seem to mark the colony's borders. Weaver ants are fierce warriors. They defend their territory against other ants, including other weaver colonies. They also attack insects and mammals that visit their trees.

WEAVER ANT LARVAE PROVIDE THE SILK TO WEAVE THE NEST TOGETHER.

Weaver ants are used as the oldest known method of biological pest control. Chinese farmers have placed weaver ant nests in citrus orchards for at least 1,700 years. The ants attack insects that damage the trees or spread diseases. Chinese farmers still do this today, instead of spraying chemical pesticides.

Honeypot Ants

The hot, dry desert of northern Mexico and the southwestern United States is not an easy place for any organism to live. Often food and water are scarce. Any creature that lives here must be able to survive these shortages. As you might expect, ants have successfully adapted to these harsh conditions.

One of the most interesting ants of the desert Southwest is the honeypot ant. These ants get some of their food from honeydew excretions of insects, and from plant nectar. This species gets the name "honeypot" from its unique way of storing that food.

SOME HONEYPOT ANTS BECOME LIVING STORAGE VESSELS.

Honeypot ants nest deep in the ground. Specialized workers serve as storage jars for any extra food. These workers are called repletes (from the word meaning "full"). Other workers feed honeydew and nectar to the repletes, who store it in their crops. Their gasters swell to the size of a large pea. Each replete becomes a translucent golden ball of honey with legs and a head.

A mature honeypot colony includes a queen, about fifteen thousand workers, and about two thousand repletes. Repletes hang by their feet from the ceiling of special storage chambers. They are so heavy that if they fall, other workers must help them climb back into place. During lean times, the repletes regurgitate the stored honey to feed the colony.

Honeypot colonies have a fascinating way of defending their territory. If one colony finds a rich food source, some of its workers will engage the workers of a rival colony in a "tournament" of aggression. Ants from the two colonies pair up, while others seem to watch. They stand high on their legs, as if measuring one another, and point their abdomens at each other. After ten to thirty seconds, each ant moves on to challenge another worker. There is almost no actual fighting. The tournament can go on for several days. Meanwhile, other workers gather the food while the ants from the rival colony are kept busy with the tournament.

If the tournament shows that one colony is much larger than the other, however, the larger colony goes to war. Its workers raid the smaller nest and kill the queen. The victors carry the larvae, pupae, newly hatched callow workers, and repletes back to their own nest. The captured ants spend the rest of their lives serving their conquerors. In short, honeypot ants capture and use slave labor.

Parasitic Ants

Honeypot ants are not the only ants to practice slavery. In fact, slavery is quite common among ants. More than two hundred different species of ants practice this kind of parasitic behavior. Some ant species cannot survive without slaves from other species. For example, European Amazon ants cannot dig nests, care for young, or even feed themselves. They rely entirely on workers, captured as pupae, from colonies of another species.

We usually think of ants as hardworking, but slave-making ants hardly work at all. Parasitic ants use a wide range of strategies to enslave other workers. In some slave-making species, the queen sneaks into a host colony, probably using false chemical signals. She then kills the host queen and takes her place. Another species, *Formica subintegra*, uses chemical warfare in its slave raids. The raiders produce pheromones that seem to panic their victims or even cause them to attack one another, while the raiders make off with larvae and pupae that will later serve them as workers.

AMAZON ANT WORKERS RAID A NEST, CAPTURING PUPAE THAT WILL SERVE AS NEW
SLAVES.

What exactly do ant slaves do? Here's how one particular
species of ants uses slavery. *Protomognathus americanus* is a
common ant in the eastern United States and Canada. It
enslaves any of three different species in the genus *Leptothorax*.
After mating, the new *P. americanus* queen finds and attacks a
Leptothorax nest. If she is successful, the *Leptothorax* queen and
workers abandon their nest. The *P. americanus* queen then takes
over the brood they leave behind. The developing larvae and
pupae emerge to serve her and her offspring as slaves.

The enslaved ants do all the work. They build the nest, forage for food, and raise the young. They even feed their mis-
tresses. The only thing the *P. americanus* workers do is raid other
nests. They attack other *Leptothorax* nests, bringing back more
larvae and pupae to maintain the slave labor in their colony. A
mature colony might have five or six slaves for each *P. americanus* worker.

8

It's an Ant's World

Athin black line creeps over a windowsill and down the kitchen wall. It crawls along the counter to a dish where someone has left a few bits of fruit. Tiny black ants, each one barely larger that a grain of pepper, scurry back and forth, touching each other's antennae as they pass. They seem never to stop or rest. Each ant carries a tiny bit of food across the counter, over the windowsill, and back to the colony, hidden somewhere inside the wall.

It's a scene repeated millions of times a day throughout the world. In the countryside, in the suburbs, and even on the upper floors of tall apartment buildings, ants and humans share the same spaces, and sometimes come into conflict with one another.

HARVESTER ANTS TRANSPORT AND PLANT MANY KINDS OF SEEDS.

Ants and the Environment

Ants play an essential part in most ecosystems. By weight and by numbers, they make up a large part of the animal life in tropical regions. In many parts of the world, ants are the leading predator of insects and other small invertebrates. In turn, they are eaten by a wide range of other animals—insects, spiders, lizards, frogs, and toads, and even a few mammals, including people.

Ants remake the world they live in to better suit their needs. And as they do, ants also affect the world's plant life. They turn over and aerate the soil, and recycle the nutrients from dead animals into fertilizer. This makes the ground more hospitable for plant growth. Harvester ants transport seeds to new locations, and plant them by carrying the seeds into their nests. Thousands of plant species around the world, including many common wildflowers, depend on ants to spread their seeds.

By preying on insects, ants greatly reduce the damage that plants would otherwise suffer. And, of course, there are ant species that protect the plants they nest in from other insects and even from competing plants. Experiments show that when the ants are removed, these trees don't grow nearly as well.

In much of Central and South America, leafcutter ants destroy about one-fifth of all the vegetation growing in the rain forest—more than any other animal of any size. They cause millions of dollars' worth of crop damage each day. On the other hand, the decomposing leaves in their underground nests enrich the rain forest soil for future plant growth.

One thing that ants do surprisingly little of is pollinating plants. Ants tend to return to the same place over and over again, instead of traveling from plant to plant. They also groom themselves frequently, removing pollen grains before they can be transferred to other flowers. And the powerful chemicals they produce may also damage pollen. So, very few plant species have developed partnerships with ants for pollination.

Conflict Between Ants and Humans

The global presence of ants mirrors that of another widespread species—our own. It seems almost inevitable that ants and humans would come into conflict. And, of course, we do. Fortunately, humans and ants do not compete for the same resources. Otherwise, it would be all-out war. And it's not hard to guess who would win that war. (Here's a hint: Which one of us has already survived for more than 100 million years?) We already know that the leafcutter ants of South and Central America can strip a farmer's field of crops. But there are other ant species that also come into conflict with people.

Carpenter ants are insect predators. They don't eat wood, but they do make their homes in it. That's not a problem in a fallen log. However, carpenter ants also settle in wooden buildings. When they do, they gradually chew their way through the wood framing as they build their nests. This weakens the building, of course. Carpenter ants prefer moist wood, so they are most often found near kitchens or bathrooms, especially around leaking pipes, gutters, and downspouts.

People rarely see carpenter ants, except when their winged forms swarm in the spring. Then they are often mistaken for termites. Carpenter ants are not nearly as damaging as termites, but when they invade a home, they must be removed before they do serious harm.

Other ant species that come into conflict with humans are Argentine ants and pharaoh ants. Both species are world travelers. They have migrated from their original habitats in South America and North Africa, hitchhiking rides on boats, trains,

ANTS CAN TRANSFORM THEIR ENVIRONMENT.

and planes. They are now found around the globe, in places where few natural predators keep their populations in check.

You may have seen tiny, foraging pharoah ants in your kitchen. They live in large colonies with multiple queens, and move their colonies frequently. Because they need warmth, they often nest between the walls of houses or even in people's belongings. Unlike most species, their queens live only a few months. Pharoah ants are difficult to control. They reproduce rapidly and spread by dividing into daughter colonies. Pharoah ants can spread disease-causing bacteria when they nest and forage in hospitals. But mostly, they're just unwanted visitors in our homes.

Argentine ants are an even greater problem. They are also small but aggressive. Argentine ants ordinarily nest outdoors, but they do enter people's homes to forage. Argentine ants form supercolonies, large groups of individual colonies whose members recognize one another and carry on their foraging without conflict. By not fighting among themselves, they have a great advantage over other species. In California, for example, they have overrun many of the native ants. The drop in other ant populations may upset the balance of an ecosystem. Birds and other creatures rely on insect prey that the Argentine invaders destroy. Other creatures—such as ant-eating lizards and plants that need ants to spread their seeds—depend on the native ants. When Argentine ants displace the native species, many other plants and animals suffer.

Another imported ant aggressor is the red fire ant. In the 1930s they reached the port of Mobile, Alabama, probably in an agricultural shipment from Brazil. Since then, red fire ants have invaded much of the southeastern United States. They have spread to at least nine states, from Florida to Texas, and as far north as Tennessee.

Fire ants build large earthen mounds more than one foot

CARPENTER ANTS CAN DO SERIOUS DAMAGE TO WOOD STRUCTURES.

(32 cm) high. They live in large colonies and reproduce rapidly. They too sometimes form supercolonies. And like the Argentine ants, they also chase out local ant species.

Fire ants cause problems when they nest in orchards, farm fields, or lawns. Their tall hard mounds damage farm machinery and their painful stings can kill young farm animals. Some people have severe allergic reactions to them. Fire ants feed on insect pests, but their mounds and their aggressive behavior make them serious pests themselves. Although an infestation of a few colonies can be controlled with insecticides, scientists haven't been able to stop their spread across the southern United States. The U.S. Department of Agriculture now requires inspections in twelve states to prevent the transport of fire ant colonies hidden in sod or nursery plants. Nevertheless, these unpleasant ants will almost certainly continue to spread until cooler or drier climates finally stop them.

Do human activities put the survival of some ant species in jeopardy? Ecologists know very little about endangered ants. But a number of species are certainly threatened by our activities, especially those living in limited areas. As tropical rain forests are cleared for timber and farmland, for example, localized species of ants lose their habitats. Some rare ant species may become extinct even before myrmecologists know they exist.

Controlling Ant Pests

How can people control ants in their homes? The most effective way is to destroy the colony, if it can be found by tracing foraging workers back to their nest. But that is usually not possible. Another solution is to make sure no food is available for the ants. Clean up spills and store food in tightly sealed containers. Sealing cracks in the walls where ants enter can also help.

People can also keep ants out of their houses by clearing trees, shrubbery, firewood, and leaves away from the outside of their homes. Home and garden shops also sell sticky substances that will help stop ants from entering buildings or climbing fruit trees. Water is an effective ant barrier. In places where ants are a nuisance, people sometimes place table legs in small cups or pans of water. The water prevents the ants from climbing up the table in search of food.

Spraying with insecticides almost never works. It kills a few workers but leaves the rest of the colony unharmed. The most effective ant poisons kill slowly. Foragers bring the slow-acting poisoned bait back to the colony to share with other workers and the queen. When the queen dies, the colony dies.

The truth is, human beings are never going to get rid of ants. Nor should we want to. Ants outnumber humans by more than a million to one. They'll almost certainly be living on Earth long after our species is gone. Probably the best thing we can do with ants is to learn more about them.

ALTHOUGH INDIVIDUAL ANTS ARE TINY, THEY PLAY A LARGE ROLE IN MOST OF THE WORLD'S ECOSYSTEMS.

Ant society works very differently from our own. We humans seem to value individual achievement and satisfaction over all else. The purpose of our society is to help each of us reach those goals. But for ants, success of the society itself is most important. The life of any one individual means almost nothing. Studying and thinking about ants may teach us something about our-selves—how and why our society was built, and how we have become a successful species. But more importantly, studying these amazing social creatures teaches us about the ants them-selves, how various animal and plant species depend on one another, and about the astounding variety of life on Earth.

Glossary

alate—having wings; winged, reproductive male or female ants

alimentary eggs—eggs that adult ants use to feed either the queen or her larvae

altruism—the act of sacrificing one's self for the good of others

amber—a clear, orange-yellow gem formed from fossilized tree sap

arthropods—large group of animals—including insects—that have jointed legs, a hard exoskeleton, and segmented bodies

bivouac—a temporary resting place or encampment

callow—a soft, pale adult ant recently emerged from a pupa

carnivorous—meat-eating

carton—cardboardlike nest-building material ants make from chewed wood pulp, saliva and bits of soil

castes—groups of ants within the colony that have different body forms for performing different tasks

chitin—the stiff material that forms the exoskeleton or outer covering of ants and other insects

chordotonal organs—small organs on the antennae, legs, trunk, and head of ants and other insects that are sensitive to sound vibrations

claustral cell—a closed chamber into which a new queen ant seals herself while she raises her first brood of workers

co-evolution—the process by which two different species evolve together, either to depend on one another, or to defend themselves against one another

crop—a reservoir in the digestive system where an ant stores food to share with nestmates; also called the social stomach

diploid—having two sets of chromosomes

diurnal—active during the day

entomology—the study of insects; a scientist who studies insects is an entomologist

exoskeleton—the stiff outer covering of ants and other insects

food bodies—small bulbs of starch, fats, and protein produced by plants that ants feed on

forage—to search for food

fossil—the remains of an ancient plant or animal preserved in stone

gaster—the rearmost section of an ant's body

genus, genera (pl.)—a group of closely related species

haploid—having a single set of chromosomes

haplodiploidy—the form of reproduction of ants, bees, and wasps, in which females have two sets of chromosomes while males, which develop from unfertilized eggs, have only one

larva, larvae (pl.)—the wormlike juvenile stage of many insects, including ants

legionary ants—another name for army ants, especially those found in the Americas

major workers—the largest workers in an ant colony; soldier ants

mandibles—the large outer jaws of an ant

maxillae—the small inner jaws of an ant

media workers—middle-sized workers in an ant colony

metamorphosis—the process by which an insect develops and changes from egg to larva to pupa to adult

midden—a place where ants deposit food remains and other waste

minor workers—the smallest-sized workers in an ant colony

mutualism—a relationship between two different species, in which both creatures benefit

myrmecology—the study of ants; A scientist who studies ants is a myrmecologist

myrmecophile—an animal that spends at least a part of its life cycle living among ants

nectaries—parts of a plant (other than flowers) that produce sweet nectar for insects to drink

nuptial flight—the mating flight of winged male and female ants

ocelli—simple eyes on top of the ant's head that can distinguish light and dark

omnivorous—eating both meat and plants

ovipositor—a tubular organ extending from the rear of a female insect's abdomen, used for depositing eggs

petiole—the narrow "waist" that connects the thorax of an ant to its gaster

pheromone—a chemical, produced in a gland, used for communication

pupa, pupae (pl.)—a resting stage during which a larvae changes into an adult

replete—full; refers to individual honeypot ants that serve as food storage vessels for the colony

reproductive males and females—male and female individuals, ordinarily winged, usually produced once a year by an ant colony, and then released to mate with individuals from other colonies

social behavior—activities carried out cooperatively by groups of ants, such as nest building, caring for larvae, foraging for food, or defending the nest

species—any particular type of organism able to reproduce more of its own kind

spermatheca—a reservoir in the gaster of an ant queen in which she stores sperm from her mating flight

spiracles—external openings in the ant's exoskeleton that allow oxygen to pass into the body and be absorbed by the blood

stridulations—sounds ants produce by rubbing ridged section on their abdomen with a scraper on their petiole

supercolony—a group of ant colonies whose members recognize one another as sisters rather than rivals

superorganism—a group of individual animals (such as the ants in a colony) that live, work, and reproduce as if they were a single creature

symbiosis—a close relationship between two different species

trophallaxis—the process by which ants feed one another with food regurgitated (spit up) from their crops

trophobiosis—the process by which ants gather food from the excretions of other insects; these insects, such as aphids, are called trophobionts

Species Checklist

In some cases, the "species" referred to in the text are actually several closely related species within a genus of ants. This is shown by using the generic name followed by the abbreviation *sp*. For example, *Azteca* sp. means several species in the genus *Azteca*.

Acacia ants (*Pseudomyrmex ferrugineus*)
> These ants live in the hollow thorns of acacia trees. The trees provide the ants with food. In return, the ants defend the trees from insects, larger animals, and even from the growth of nearby plants.

Amazon ants (*Polyergus rufescens*)
> A European slave-making species of ant.

Argentine ants (*Linepithema humilis*)
> Originally from South America, these ants have traveled by ship, train, and plane and now live almost everywhere on Earth. In some places, they may displace native ant species and change the balance of the local ecosystem. (Previously known as Iridomyrmex humilis.)

Asian carpenter ant (*Camponotus saundersi*)
> This species of Asian carpenter ant defends its colony by bursting and spraying attackers with poison.

Aztec ant (*Azteca* sp.)
> These ants live in the hollow stems of cecropia trees. The trees provide the ants with most of their food. In return, the ants defend the trees from insects and larger animals

Bulldog ants (*Myrmecia* sp.)
> Large primitive ants native to Australia. These ants have powerful stings, and can jump several inches when defending their small colonies.

Bullet ant or Bala (*Paraponera clavata*)
> Large ants of Central and South American rain forests, with very painful stings.

Carpenter ants (*Camponotus* sp.)
> Ants that build their homes in damp and rotting wood. Because of their nesting behavior, they can damage homes, and are sometimes mistaken for termites.

Eciton burchelli
> The most familiar army ant of the Central and South American rain forest. These ants make no permanent home. The colonies of about five hundred thousand ants move from place to place, preying on insects and other small creatures in their path.

Formica subintegra
> An American slave-making species of ant that uses pheromones to panic and confuse the victims of their raids.

Formica yessensis
> A Japanese species of ant that creates huge supercolonies with multiple queens.

Harvester ants (*Pogonomyrmex* sp.)
> These ants build underground nests, and gather plant seeds for food. They also help plants by transporting seeds to new locations, where they sprout.

Honeypot ants (*Myremecocystus* sp.)
> Honeypot ants live in the desert regions of northern Mexico and the southwestern United States. They store food in the crops of workers—called repletes—which hang from the ceilings of their nests like golden balls of honey.

Leafcutter ants (*Atta* sp. and *Acromyrmex* sp.)
> These ants harvest and chew up the leaves of many different plants. They then grow fungus in the leafy compost for food.

Leptothorax sp.
> Common and widespread genus of ant. Three *Leptothorax* species—*Leptothorax ambiguous*, *Leptothorax curvispinosus* and *Leptothorax longispinosus*—are parasitized by Protomognathus americanus.

Pharaoh ants (*Monomorium pharaonis*)
> These tropical stinging ants now live almost everywhere on Earth. They are frequently found in the walls of homes and other buildings.

Protomognathus americanus
> A variety of ant that lives in the eastern United States and Canada. These ants enslave members of other species (*Leptothorax* sp.), who then do almost all the work of maintaining their nest.

Red harvester ants (*Pogonomyrmex barbatus*)
> A common harvester ant species of the desert area of the American Southwest. They are large ants, about 0.4 inches (1 cm).

Red imported fire ants (*Solenopsis invicta*)
> These stinging ants, originally from Brazil, were accidentally brought to Mobile, Alabama, in the 1930s. Since then, they have spread across most of the southeastern United States, and become a serious agricultural pest.

Weaver ants (*Oecophylla sp.*)
> These residents of tropical Africa, Asia, and Australia live in trees. They build nests by weaving leaves together with the silk from their larvae.

Further Research

A tremendous amount has been written about ants. Here you will find a list of books, videos, organizations, and Websites to get you started.

Books for Young People

Fischer-Nagel, Heiderose. *An Ant Colony*. Translated from the German by Gerd Kirchner. Minneapolis: Carolrhoda Books, 1989

Lesinski, Jeanne M. *Exotic Invaders: Killer Bees, Fire Ants, and Other Alien Species Are Infesting America!* New York: Walker and Co., 1996.

Overbeck, Cynthia. *Ants* (Lerner Natural Science). Minneapolis: Lerner Publications Company, 1988.

Parramon, Jose M., Angels Julivert, and Marcel Socias. *The Fascinating World of Ants*. Hauppauge, NY: Barron's Educational Series, 1991.

Pascoe, Elaine. *Ants* (Nature Close-Up). Woodbridge, CT: Blackbirch Marketing, 1998.

Settel, Joanne. *Exploding Ants: Amazing Facts About How Animals Adapt*. New York: Atheneum, 1999.

Simon, Seymour. *Deadly Ants*. New York: Four Winds Press, 1979.

Steele, Christy. *Ants* (Animals of the Rain Forest Series). Austin, TX: Raintree Steck-Vaughn Publishers, 2000.

Stefoff, Rebecca. *Ant* (*Living Things* series). Tarrytown, NY: Benchmark Books, 1998.

Van Woerkom, Dorothy. *Hidden Messages*. New York: Crown Publishers, 1979.

Watts, Barrie. *Ants*. New York: Franklin Watts, 1990.

Videos

Little Creatures Who Run the World, NOVA, WGBH/Boston, 1995.
The Ultimate Guide to Ants, The Discovery Channel.

Organizations

Association of Ant Colony Developers 55 Chinkaberry Ct., Howell, NJ 07731; phone: 732-431-4440; Website: http://www.antcolony.org

Young Entomologists' Society, Inc. 6907 West Grand River Ave., Lansing MI 48906-9131 Phone/Fax: 517-886-0630; E-mail: YESbugs@aol.com; Website: http://members.aol.com/YESbugs/mainmenu.html

Web Sites

Myrmecology: The Scientific Study of Ants
http://www.myrmecology.org

Social Insects World Wide Web SIWeb
http://research.amnh.org/entomology/social_insects/index.html

The Ants of West Africa
http://ibis.nott.ac.ui/~plzbt/wafants/antcover.htm

Ants of Costa Rica
    http://www.evergreen.edu/user/ser_res/research/arthropod/AntsofCostaRica.html.
Smithsonian Institution Dept. of Entomology Ant database
    http://160.111.87.10:591/entomology/siants/search.html
The Amazing World of Ants
    http://www.earthlife.net/insects/ants.html
Ants of Florida
    http://edis.ifas.ufl.edu/scripts/htmlgen.exe?DOCUMENT IG080
The Ant Farm
    http://home.apu.edu/~philpi/antfarm/antfarm.html
Fire ant information from Texas A&M University
    http://fireant.tamu.edu

Bibliography

These books were used by the author in his research. They offer more detailed information at an adult reading level.

Beattie, Andrew J. *The Evolutionary Ecology of Ant-Plant Mutualisms* (Cambridge Studies in Ecology). Cambridge, U.K.: Cambridge University Press, 1985.

Bourke, Andrew F. G., and Nigel R. Franks. *Social Evolution in Ants*. Princeton, NJ: Princeton University Press, 1995.

Gordon, Deborah M. *Ants at Work: How an Insect Society is Organized*. New York: Free Press, 1999.

Hölldobler, Bert, and Edward O. Wilson. *The Ants*. Cambridge: Harvard University Press, 1990.

———. *Journey to the Ants*. Cambridge: The Belknap Press of the Harvard University Press, 1994.

Hoyt, Erich. *The Earth Dwellers: Adventures in the Land of the Ants*. New York: Simon and Schuster, 1996.

Newman, L. Hugh. *Ants From Close Up*. New York: Thomas Y. Crowell, 1967.

Taber, Stephen Welton. *Fire Ants*. College Station: Texas A&M University Press, 2000.

———. *The World of the Harvester Ants* (W.L. Moody, Jr., Natural History Series, No. 23). College Station: Texas A&M University Press, 1998.

Wheeler, William M. *Ants Their Structure, Development, and Behavior*. Revised ed. New York: Columbia University Press, 1960.

Index

Page numbers for illustrations are in **boldface**.

About the Author

PAUL FLEISHER has taught in Richmond's Programs for the Gifted since 1978. He has published numerous books for young people on scientific topics. He has also written several pieces of educational software, one of which, *Perplexing Puzzles*, won a Parent's Choice Award in 1985.

Mr. Fleisher is active in various organizations working for peace and social justice. In 1988 he received the Virginia Education Association's Award for Peace and International Relations, and in 1999 he was awarded the Thomas Jefferson Medal for Outstanding Contributions to Natural Science Education.

He lives with his wife, Debra Sims Fleisher, and can often be found working in his garden or fishing on the Chesapeake Bay.